Prometheus and the Story of Fire

Written by I. M. Richardson
Illustrated by Robert Baxter

Troll Associates

Library of Congress Cataloging in Publication Data

Richardson, I. M.
    Prometheus and the story of fire.

    Summary: Relates how the Titan Prometheus created
people, gave them fire he stole from the gods, and was
horribly punished by Zeus.
    1. Prometheus (Greek mythology)—Juvenile literature.
[1. Prometheus (Greek mythology)   2. Mythology,
Greek]   I. Baxter, Robert, 1930-   ill.   II. Title.
BL820.P68R5   1983   292'.211   82-15979
ISBN 0-89375-859-0
ISBN 0-89375-860-4 (pbk.)

The myths and legends of Ancient Greece tell of powerful Titans, mighty gods and goddesses, heroes, monsters, and mortals. Where did they all come from? The answers are here, in the story of Prometheus and Pandora. Prometheus was an immortal—the wisest of the Titans. Pandora was a mortal—the first woman. But their story begins long before there were any gods or people.

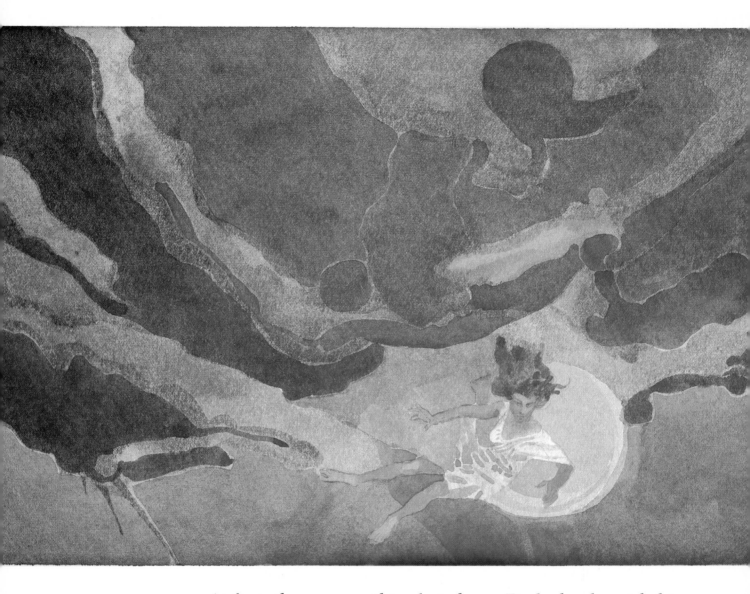

At first, there was nothing but chaos. Dark clouds swirled in an endless sea of emptiness. Then Gaea, or mother earth, appeared. High above her was Uranus, or the sky, with his crown of stars. According to legend, Gaea and Uranus had many children.

Their first children were monsters. These terrible creatures had fifty heads and a hundred hands. Each was more powerful than a hurricane and mightier than a thousand volcanoes. They used thunder, lightning, and earthquakes as their weapons.

But these monsters were not alone in the world. There were three other monsters, who were also the children of Gaea and Uranus. Each of these monsters was known as a Cyclops. Instead of two eyes, each Cyclops had only one—a single, gigantic eye right in the middle of its forehead. Each mighty Cyclops was as tall as a mountain.

6

The brothers and sisters of these many monsters were called
Titans. The Titans were huge and powerful. Although they
were not as ugly or destructive as the monsters, the Titans were
not as wise as the gods who came later. Only Prometheus, who
was the son of one of the first Titans, would be known for his
great wisdom.

The Titans wandered freely throughout the world. Sometimes they came upon a Cyclops, but they never saw their other brothers—the monsters with fifty heads. Their father, Uranus, had locked these ugly creatures in an underground prison. This angered their mother, Gaea. She asked all her other children to help free their fifty-headed brothers.

At first, no one was brave enough to try. But then the Titan named Cronus came forward. "I will challenge my father and free my brothers," he boldly announced. But what Cronus really wanted was to seize control of the universe from his father.

Cronus overthrew his father and became Lord of the Universe. But he did not release the monsters with fifty heads. He married a Titan named Rhea, and they had five children. But Cronus feared that someday one of his children would overthrow him. To prevent this, he swallowed each child. But since all Titans are immortal and cannot die, the children grew up inside him.

When they had a sixth child, Rhea named him Zeus. She secretly sent him off to be raised by the nymphs on the island of Crete. Then she wrapped a rock in the baby's blanket and gave it to her husband. Cronus thought the rock was the newborn child, and he promptly swallowed it.

As Zeus grew up, he became more and more powerful. One day, his mother told him how his father had swallowed Zeus's brothers and sisters. At once, Zeus formed a plan to challenge Cronus. With the help of his grandmother, Gaea, he freed his brothers and sisters. They had grown up, and now they were as powerful as their father.

A huge and terrible war followed. On one side were the Titans, led by Cronus. On the other side were the children of Cronus, the gods led by mighty Zeus. It was a dreadful, destructive war, and it rocked the world. It probably would have destroyed the universe, if not for the wisdom of Prometheus.

Prometheus was wise enough to know that Zeus would win the war. So he joined forces with Zeus and advised him to release the monsters with the fifty heads. Soon the monsters raged about, hurling their terrible weapons against Cronus. When it was over, the gods had won, and Zeus had taken lightning as his personal weapon.

The gods and goddesses went to the top of Mount Olympus, which became their home. They divided the universe among themselves, and Zeus became the supreme ruler. One day, he decided that it was time for animals and people to appear. He gave the job to Prometheus, whose name means "forethought," and to the brother of Prometheus, Epimetheus.

Unfortunately, Epimetheus, whose name means "afterthought," was not very bright. He wandered around, giving all the best gifts to the animals. He gave out courage and cunning, speed and strength. He gave out feathers and claws, wings and shells. Then, when it was time for people to be made, he realized that there were no good gifts left.

Now Prometheus took over the job. He gave people a different shape from animals. He gave them two legs instead of four, so they could stand up straight. Then, still pitying them, he thought of a special gift for the human race. He would give mortals something far better than wings or claws—he would give them the gift of fire.

Fire would be a valuable gift. With fire, people would be able to light up the night, cook their food, warm themselves, and frighten away wild animals. But fire belonged to the gods. Prometheus would have to steal it! Athena, the goddess of wisdom, showed him how to enter Olympus, the home of the gods.

Prometheus had brought with him a hollow reed. He crept up to the sacred hearth, and when no one was looking, he hid a glowing ember of fire inside the reed. Then, before any of the gods realized what had happened, he slipped away. He returned to earth at once and gave fire to mortals.

Zeus was furious! He would think of a way to punish
Prometheus for stealing fire. But first, he would punish the
mortals for accepting the gift. Their punishment would be
brought by Pandora—the first woman. The task of making
Pandora was given to Hephaestus, the god of fire. But each of
the other gods contributed something.

Aphrodite, the goddess of love, gave Pandora grace and charm, so no mortal could resist her. Apollo gave her the gift of music. Athena gave her wisdom. Hermes, the messenger of the gods, gave her the valuable gift of persuasion. And someone—perhaps it was Zeus himself—filled her with curiosity.

Then each of the gods put something into a beautiful golden box, and Zeus closed the lid tightly. He gave the box to Pandora and told her that she was never to open it. Then he sent her down into the world to Epimetheus.

Prometheus had told his brother that he should never accept any gifts from Zeus. But when Epimetheus saw Pandora, he quickly forgot his brother's warning. The charms of this woman were so great that Epimetheus fell in love with her at once and took her for his wife.

It wasn't long before Pandora's curiosity brought terrible problems down upon the human race. "I must know what is inside this box," she said. "Since it comes from the gods, it must contain something splendid." Her curiosity grew and grew. Finally, she could not stand it any longer, and she peeked inside.

As soon as the box was opened, a thousand miseries flew out. Among them were envy and greed, injustice and prejudice, famine and disease. They swarmed out and swirled away, carried by the winds to the far corners of the earth. Pandora slammed the lid shut, but the miserable evils had already escaped. Only hope remained in the box. And to this day, hope never leaves us.

Now Zeus turned his attention to the punishment of Prometheus. Because Prometheus was a Titan, he could never be killed. But Zeus thought of a punishment that was worse than death. He said, "Just as his life has no end, so will his suffering have no end." Then he called up Force and Violence, his mighty servants.

He told them to seize Prometheus and take him far away, to Mount Caucasus. There, Zeus chained Prometheus to a rock, saying, "You dared to steal from the gods and you must be punished. From now until eternity, you shall have no rest, no sleep, no peace." And then mighty Zeus returned to Mount Olympus.

According to the Fates, who decided what was to be, there was only one way Zeus could be overthrown. If he married a certain goddess, and if they had a son, the child would one day overthrow his father. Zeus wanted to know who the goddess was, but only Prometheus knew. Zeus offered to free him in exchange for the secret. But the Titan refused to tell.

28

As time passed, Zeus became more and more anxious and impatient. One day, he sent Hermes to Prometheus. "If you do not reveal the secret," said Hermes, "your punishment will become a thousand times worse than it is now." But still, Prometheus would not speak.

From that day on, Prometheus suffered as no one had ever suffered before. Zeus sent a huge and terrible eagle, who landed on the rock next to Prometheus. Each day, the eagle tore at Prometheus's liver. And each night, it grew back, so the eagle could tear it out again the next day.

Generations passed, but even this horrible torture did not weaken the will of Prometheus. In spite of his suffering, he was determined not to give in to Zeus. Finally, Hercules set him free. Hercules was one of the many sons of Zeus and the strongest hero the world has ever known. He killed the eagle and broke the chains that bound Prometheus to the rock.

Prometheus had helped Zeus win the war against the Titans. Out of pity, he had stolen fire from the gods and given it to people as a gift. He had endured long and terrible suffering without giving in to the will of Zeus. For although his body had been chained, his spirit had always been free.